The Future Of American Democracy

'Challenges and Opportunities'

K. Bell

Disclaimer

The information contained in this book "The Future of American Democracy: Challenges and Opportunities" is intended to provide general guidance on effective American politics. The views and opinions expressed in this content are solely those of the author and do not necessarily reflect the official policy or position of any organization or institution mentioned

The author and publisher of this book are not responsible for any errors or omissions, or any actions taken based on the information presented in this book. The reader is solely responsible for their actions and should seek professional advice if necessary.

Table of Contents.

Abstract

In recent years, American democracy has faced unprecedented challenges. From the 2016 presidential election, which was marred by allegations of foreign interference and voter suppression, to the storming of the Capitol in 2021, which shook the foundations of our political system, it's clear that our democracy is under threat. But in the face of these challenges, there's also reason for hope. Grassroots movements, civic engagement, and innovative technology are all driving forces for positive change in our democracy.

In this article, we'll explore the state of American democracy today, examining the challenges and opportunities that lie ahead. We'll start by taking a hard look at the threats to democracy, including polarization, disinformation, and voter suppression. From there, we'll dive into the opportunities for reform, exploring topics such as voting rights, campaign finance, and more.

But this isn't just a theoretical discussion. The future of American democracy is on the line, and it's up to all of us to help shape that future. Whether we're talking about voting in elections, participating in protests and movements, or simply staying informed about the issues that matter most, every one of us has a role to play in strengthening our democracy.

As we embark on this journey, it's important to remember that the challenges facing our democracy are complex and multifaceted. There are no easy answers or quick fixes, but by working together and staying committed to our values, we can create a more just, equitable, and sustainable democracy for all.

So join us as we explore the challenges and opportunities that lie ahead, and let's work together to build a brighter future for American democracy.

Chapter 1

I. Introduction: The Current State of American Democracy

American democracy is facing unprecedented challenges in the modern era. The United States, once viewed as a beacon of democracy and freedom, is now grappling with significant threats to the very foundations of our political system. From the rise of authoritarianism and the erosion of democratic norms to the influence of special interests and voter suppression, numerous challenges must be addressed if we are to preserve our democratic ideals.

The polarization of American politics has reached new heights, with each side seeing the other as not just opponents, but as enemies. Political discourse has become increasingly divisive, with a focus on "winning" rather than governing. This has resulted in a lack of compromise and a failure to address critical issues facing our country.

Furthermore, disinformation and propaganda have become pervasive in our political discourse, with some politicians and media outlets pushing their agenda and narratives, rather than focusing on facts and truth. This has created an environment in which it is difficult for citizens to make informed decisions and has led to deep divisions within the electorate.

In addition, voter suppression efforts aimed at marginalized communities threaten to undermine the very foundation of our democracy. These efforts range from strict voter ID laws to reducing early voting days and closing polling places, making it more difficult for people to exercise their right to vote.

The events of January 6, 2021, when a mob of Trump supporters stormed the Capitol in an attempt to overturn the election, have underscored just how urgent it is that we address these challenges. It's clear that our democracy is at a critical juncture, and the future of American democracy hangs in the balance.

But despite these challenges, there is reason for hope. Across the country, grassroots movements are working to create positive change and strengthen our democracy. From efforts to increase voter turnout and reform campaign finance laws to initiatives aimed at restoring trust in our institutions, there are many opportunities for reform and renewal.

In the following sections, we'll explore the challenges and opportunities facing American democracy, and we'll discuss what each of us can do to help ensure that our democracy endures. We'll look at some of the key issues facing our democracy today, and examine how we can work together to create a brighter future for all Americans.

II. Threats to Democracy: Polarization, Disinformation, and Voter Suppression

American democracy is facing several significant challenges, including polarization, disinformation, and voter suppression. These threats are interconnected, and they pose a serious risk to the integrity of our political system.

Polarization has become one of the most visible and troubling challenges to American democracy in recent years. The political divide in America has deepened to the point where people on opposite sides of the political spectrum view each other not just as opponents, but as enemies. This has created an environment in which compromise is seen as a weakness and political discourse has become increasingly vitriolic and divisive.

Polarization is fueled in part by the way that we consume media. Many Americans now get their news from sources that confirm their existing beliefs, creating what has been referred to as an "echo chamber" effect. This makes it difficult to have productive conversations about policy, and it reinforces pre-existing biases rather than challenging them.

Disinformation is another significant threat to American democracy. The internet and social media have made it easier than ever for false or misleading information to spread quickly and easily. From foreign interference in our elections to domestic propaganda, disinformation undermines the ability of citizens to make informed decisions and it erodes trust in our institutions. If we cannot agree on what is true, how can we expect to have a functioning democracy?

Voter suppression is a direct attack on the foundation of American democracy. When eligible voters are prevented from participating in elections, either through strict voter ID laws or other means, we risk creating a system where only certain voices are heard. This undermines the legitimacy of our government and can lead to a dangerous cycle of mistrust and unrest.

Voter suppression has historically been aimed at marginalized communities, including people of color, low-income Americans, and young people. These communities are more likely to face barriers to voting, such as strict voter ID laws or the closure of polling places in their neighborhoods. When these communities are unable to participate fully in the political process, their interests are often ignored by elected officials.

The threats posed by polarization, disinformation, and voter suppression are significant, but they are not insurmountable. There are several steps that we can take to address these challenges and strengthen our democracy.

First, we must work to bridge the political divide and foster more productive conversations about policy. This means seeking out diverse perspectives and engaging in respectful dialogue, even with those with whom we disagree.

Second, we must combat disinformation by supporting quality journalism and fact-checking efforts. We can also take steps to educate ourselves about media literacy and how to distinguish reliable sources from those that are unreliable or propagandistic.

Finally, we must fight voter suppression by supporting efforts to expand access to the ballot box. This includes advocating for measures like automatic voter registration, early voting, and no-excuse absentee voting, as well as opposing laws and policies that restrict voting rights.

Polarization, disinformation, and voter suppression pose serious threats to American democracy. But by working together to address these challenges, we can help ensure that our political system remains strong, vibrant, and responsive to the needs of all Americans.

III.   Opportunities for Reform: Voting Rights, Campaign Finance, and More

While the threats to American democracy are significant, several opportunities for reform can help to strengthen our political system and ensure that it is more responsive to the needs of all citizens.

One of the most important areas for reform is voting rights. As mentioned earlier, voter suppression is a direct threat to American democracy, and efforts to expand access to the ballot box are essential for ensuring that all eligible voters can participate fully in our political process. This includes measures like automatic voter registration, early voting, and no-excuse absentee voting, as well as efforts to combat voter intimidation and other forms of suppression.

Another key area for reform is campaign finance. The current system of financing political campaigns is often seen as tilted in favor of wealthy donors and special interests, which can drown out the voices of ordinary citizens. Several potential reforms could help to address this issue, including public financing of campaigns, stricter limits on contributions, and greater transparency and accountability for donors.

In addition to these issues, there are several other areas where reform could help to strengthen American democracy. For example, many advocates have called for changes to our system of redistricting, which can often lead to gerrymandering and the distortion of electoral outcomes. Others have suggested reforms to the Electoral College, which can result in presidential candidates winning the popular vote but losing the election.

There are also opportunities for reform in areas like the media and civic education. Ensuring that Americans are well-informed about the issues facing our democracy and how our political system works is essential for creating an engaged and informed citizenry. This includes promoting media literacy, supporting quality journalism, and investing in civic education programs in schools and communities.

The opportunities for reform are vast, but they will require sustained and collective effort on the part of citizens, advocates, and elected officials. It will also require a willingness to engage in respectful dialogue and compromise, even on issues where there may be strong disagreements. By working together to build a stronger, more inclusive, and more responsive democracy, we can help to ensure that the American experiment in self-government continues to thrive for generations to come.

The challenges facing American democracy are real and significant, but they are not insurmountable. By focusing on opportunities for reform in areas like voting rights, campaign finance, and civic education, we can help to create a more just, equitable, and responsive political system. This will require commitment, dedication, and hard work, but the rewards of a stronger democracy will be well worth the effort.

IV. The Future of American Democracy: Where Do We Go from Here?

As we look ahead to the future of American democracy, there are many questions and uncertainties. How will we address the threats to our political system, and what opportunities for reform will we pursue? What role will citizens, advocates, and officials play in shaping the future of our democracy? And how will we navigate the complex and evolving landscape of American politics in the years and decades to come?

One thing is clear: the future of American democracy will depend on the choices we make today. We have the power to shape the direction of our political system, address the challenges facing our democracy, and told a stronger, more inclusive, and more responsive political system for future generations.

One key area where we must focus our efforts is on promoting civic engagement and participation. Democracy depends on the active involvement of citizens in the political process, and we must do more to encourage and support this involvement. This includes promoting voter registration and turnout, as well as engaging citizens in other forms of civic participation, such as volunteering, advocacy, and community organizing.

Another critical area for the future of American democracy is addressing the deep divisions and polarization that have come to define our politics in recent years. This will require a concerted effort to bridge the partisan divide, to find common ground, and to work together towards common goals. It will also require a commitment to listening to and understanding the perspectives and experiences of others, even when we may disagree with them.

At the same time, we must continue to work towards reform in areas like voting rights, campaign finance, and redistricting, as well as efforts to combat disinformation and protect the integrity of our elections. These are complex and challenging issues, but they are also essential for the health and vitality of our political system.

Another key area for the future of American democracy is promoting diversity, equity, and inclusion. Our political system must reflect the rich diversity of our nation, and we must work to ensure that all citizens have an equal voice and equal opportunities to participate in the political process. This includes addressing issues like voter suppression, gerrymandering, and other forms of discrimination, as well as promoting diversity and inclusion in all aspects of our political system.

As we navigate the future of American democracy, we must also be mindful of the global context in which our political system operates. The rise of authoritarianism, populism, and other challenges to democracy around the world highlights the importance of promoting and protecting democratic values and institutions. This includes working with international partners to promote democracy and human rights, as well as addressing global challenges like climate change, economic inequality, and conflict.

The future of American democracy will depend on our ability to come together as a nation and to work towards common goals. This will require a commitment to listening to and understanding the perspectives and experiences of others, even when we may disagree with them. It will also require a willingness to engage in respectful dialogue and compromise, even on issues where there may be strong disagreements.

As citizens, we have a critical role to play in shaping the future of American democracy. By engaging in the political process, promoting civic engagement and participation, and working towards reforms that strengthen our political system, we can help to build a brighter future for ourselves and future generations.

Together, we can ensure that the American experiment in self-government continues to thrive for centuries to come.

Chapter 2.

I. Democracy Under Fire: Challenges Facing America Today

Democracy is the foundation of American governance, but it is currently facing unprecedented challenges. From political polarization to disinformation to voter suppression, these challenges threaten the very essence of democracy. As a result, it is critical to take a hard look at the challenges facing American democracy today and consider potential solutions.

One of the most pressing challenges is political polarization. The country is more politically divided than ever before, with each side viewing the other as an existential threat. This has led to a situation where elected officials are more concerned with scoring political points than working together to solve the nation's problems. The result is a government that is gridlocked and unable to effectively address the challenges facing the country.

Another major challenge is disinformation. The proliferation of social media has made it easier than ever to spread false information, and some political actors have taken advantage of this to spread lies and undermine trust in democratic institutions. The result is a citizenry that is misinformed and distrustful, making it difficult to build consensus on important issues.

Voter suppression is yet another challenge facing American democracy. Some states have implemented policies that make it harder for certain groups of people, particularly minorities and low-income individuals, to exercise their right to vote. This undermines the fundamental principle of one person, one vote, and threatens the legitimacy of the entire democratic process.

The COVID-19 pandemic has also highlighted the fragility of American democracy. The pandemic has forced many states to implement emergency measures, such as expanded mail-in voting, to ensure that citizens can vote safely. However, some political actors have used the pandemic as an excuse to cast doubt on the legitimacy of the election results.

Given these challenges, it is clear that the future of American democracy is uncertain.

However, some steps can be taken to address these challenges and strengthen the democratic process. One potential solution is to focus on building consensus and promoting bipartisanship. Elected officials need to prioritize the needs of the country over their political careers and work together to find solutions to the challenges facing the nation.

Another solution is to invest in civic education. Citizens need to understand the importance of democracy and how it works in making informed decisions and holding elected officials accountable. This can be done through programs that teach civics and government in schools, as well as public awareness campaigns.

However, it is critical to protect the right to vote. This means implementing policies that make it easier, not harder, for citizens to exercise their right to vote. It also means holding accountable those who seek to undermine the democratic process through voter suppression and disinformation.

Finally, the challenges facing American democracy today are significant, but they are not insurmountable. By working together, investing in civic education, and protecting the right to vote, it is possible to strengthen American democracy and ensure that it continues to serve as a beacon of freedom and democracy for generations to come.

II. The People's Power: Grassroots Movements and Citizen Engagement

One of the key strengths of American democracy is the ability of ordinary citizens to come together and advocate for change. Grassroots movements and citizen engagement have played a critical role in shaping our nation's history, from the civil rights movement to the fight for marriage equality. Today, there is a wide range of grassroots movements and citizen-led initiatives working to address some of the most pressing issues facing our society.

Grassroots movements are typically defined as efforts by ordinary citizens to promote change at the local, state, or national level. These movements can take many forms, including advocacy campaigns, protests, sit-ins, and other forms of direct action. Some of the most notable grassroots movements in recent years include the Women's March, the Black Lives Matter movement, and the climate justice movement.

One of the key benefits of grassroots movements is their ability to give voice to marginalized and underrepresented communities. Grassroots movements often emerge from communities that have been historically excluded from the political process, such as people of color, women, and members of the LGBTQ+ community. These movements can help to amplify the voices of these communities and bring attention to their concerns and needs.

Another important aspect of grassroots movements is their ability to inspire and mobilize citizens. Grassroots movements often rely on the power of collective action and social solidarity to achieve their goals. By working together towards a shared vision of change, grassroots movements can create a sense of empowerment and agency among participants, helping them to see themselves as active agents of change rather than passive observers.

Citizen engagement is another critical component of American democracy. This refers to the ordinary citizens participating in the political process, including through voting, advocacy, and other forms of civic engagement. Strong citizen engagement is essential for maintaining a healthy and vibrant democracy, as it helps to ensure that elected officials are accountable to the people they represent.

There are many different ways that citizens can engage with the political process. Voting is perhaps the most important form of citizen engagement, as it provides individuals with a direct say in who is elected to represent them. Other forms of civic engagement include volunteering, participating in protests or demonstrations, signing petitions, and contacting elected officials to express support or opposition to specific policies or legislation.

Social media has also emerged as a powerful tool for citizen engagement in recent years. Platforms like Twitter, Facebook, and Instagram have made it easier than ever for citizens to connect with political leaders and organizations. Social media has been used to mobilize support for a wide range of issues, from gun control to immigration reform to climate justice.

One of the key benefits of citizen engagement is its ability to hold elected officials accountable. When citizens are engaged and active in the political process, they are better able to monitor the actions of their elected representatives and hold them accountable for their decisions. This can help to ensure that elected officials are acting in the best interests of their constituents and not simply pursuing their political agendas.

Grassroots movements and citizen engagement are essential components of American democracy. By working together to promote change and hold elected officials accountable, citizens can help to ensure that our political system remains vibrant, inclusive, and responsive to the needs of all Americans.

Whether through participation in grassroots movements, voting, or other forms of civic engagement, each of us has the power to make a difference in shaping the future of our democracy.

III. Technology and the Future of Democracy: Innovation or Obstruction?

Technology has transformed every aspect of our lives, including the way we participate in democracy. From social media to online voting, technology has the potential to make the democratic process more accessible, transparent, and efficient. At the same time, however, technology also poses new challenges and risks to the integrity of our democratic institutions. In this section, we will explore the opportunities and risks that technology presents for the future of democracy.

One of the most significant opportunities presented by technology is the ability to connect people from all over the world in real-time. Social media platforms like Facebook, Twitter, and Instagram have made it easier than ever for people to share information and ideas, organize campaigns, and mobilize support for political causes. This has the potential to make the democratic process more inclusive and accessible, as people can participate in the political process from anywhere with an internet connection.

Another way that technology is transforming democracy is through the use of big data and analytics. By analyzing large amounts of data, political campaigns can target their messages and resources more effectively, reaching the voters who are most likely to be swayed by their message. This can help to make campaigns more efficient and cost-effective, and it can also make the democratic process more responsive to the needs and desires of voters.

However, technology also poses significant risks to the future of democracy. One of the most pressing concerns is the spread of disinformation and fake news. Social media platforms have been used to spread false and misleading information, often to influence political outcomes. This can erode trust in democratic institutions and make it more difficult for citizens to make informed decisions.

Another risk associated with technology is the potential for hacking and cyber attacks. In recent years, there have been numerous reports of foreign governments and other malicious actors attempting to interfere with democratic processes through cyber attacks. This can compromise the integrity of elections and undermine public confidence in democratic institutions.

Finally, there are also concerns about the impact of technology on privacy and surveillance. As more and more information is shared online, there is a risk that governments and other organizations could use this information to monitor and control citizens. This could undermine the principles of democracy and threaten individual liberties.

Despite these risks, there is still reason for optimism about the potential of technology to support and strengthen democracy. By investing in technology that is secure, transparent, and accessible, we can harness the power of innovation to make the democratic process more inclusive and responsive. For example, some countries have experimented with online voting systems that use blockchain technology to ensure that votes are secure and transparent.

In addition to technological innovation, other steps can be taken to strengthen democracy in the digital age. For example, media literacy programs can help to educate citizens about how to identify and avoid fake news and disinformation. Strong cybersecurity measures can help to protect the integrity of democratic institutions from cyber-attacks. And efforts to promote transparency and accountability in government can help to ensure that citizens have the information they need to make informed decisions.

The future of democracy is intimately tied to the role of technology. While there are significant risks associated with the use of technology in the democratic process, there are also opportunities for innovation and progress.

By embracing technology that is secure, transparent, and inclusive, and by taking steps to mitigate the risks associated with technology, we can help to ensure that the democratic process remains strong and resilient for years to come.

IV. Building a Stronger Democracy: Lessons from the Past and Paths to the Future

The United States has a long and complex history when it comes to democracy. From the founding of the nation to the present day, there have been countless challenges and triumphs in the ongoing struggle to build a stronger, more inclusive democratic system. In this section, we will explore the lessons that can be learned from the past, as well as the paths that can be taken to build a stronger democracy for the future.

One of the most important lessons from the past is the need for broad-based participation in the democratic process. Throughout American history, there have been countless movements for political and social change, ranging from the suffrage movement to the civil rights movement to the contemporary movements for climate justice and racial equality. These movements have been successful because they have been driven by the participation of ordinary people, who have organized, mobilized, and demanded change.

Another key lesson from the past is the importance of building strong institutions that can withstand the pressures of partisanship and polarization. The Constitution was designed to create a system of checks and balances that would prevent any one branch of government from becoming too powerful. This system has been tested throughout American history, from the Civil War to the Watergate scandal to the impeachment of President Trump, and has ultimately proven resilient.

However, there are also significant challenges facing American democracy today, including polarization, disinformation, and voter suppression. These challenges threaten to undermine the very foundations of our democratic system and require urgent action if we are to build a stronger democracy for the future.

One path to a stronger democracy is to prioritize the protection and expansion of voting rights. Voter suppression tactics, such as gerrymandering and restrictive voter ID laws, have been used to prevent certain groups of people from exercising their right to vote. By implementing policies that make it easier, not harder, to vote, such as automatic voter registration and early voting, we can ensure that every citizen has an equal say in our democracy.

Another path to a stronger democracy is to reform our campaign finance system. The Supreme Court's Citizens United decision in 2010 opened the floodgates for unlimited corporate and special interest spending in elections, which has had a corrupting influence on our political system. By implementing public financing of elections and limiting the influence of big money in politics, we can help to ensure that elected officials are accountable to the people, not to wealthy donors.

In addition to these specific policy proposals, there are also broader cultural and social changes that can help to strengthen American democracy. For example, we need to foster a culture of civic engagement that encourages people to participate in the democratic process and to hold their elected officials accountable. We also need to promote media literacy and critical thinking skills so that citizens are better equipped to navigate the complex landscape of modern politics.

Building a stronger democracy requires a commitment from all of us, as individuals and as a society. It requires us to recognize the value of democracy as a system of government that allows us to come together to solve our common problems. It requires us to be vigilant in defending our democratic institutions from those who would seek to undermine them. And it requires us to be proactive in building a more inclusive and equitable democracy for the future.

The path to a stronger democracy is not an easy one, but it is a necessary one. By learning from the lessons of the past and embracing the opportunities of the future, we can build a democracy that is more responsive, more inclusive, and more resilient.

Whether through policies that expand voting rights and limit the influence of big money in politics, or through cultural changes that promote civic engagement and critical thinking, we all have a role to play in building a stronger democracy for ourselves and future generations.

Chapter 3

I. Crisis Point: The Urgent Need for Action

The United States of America is at a critical point in its history. Our democratic system, once a beacon of hope for the world, is facing unprecedented challenges that threaten to undermine its very foundations. From the rise of authoritarianism to the spread of disinformation to the erosion of civil liberties, several factors have contributed to the current crisis.

One of the key drivers of the crisis is the growing polarization of American society. The political divide between left and right has become so deep that it seems to be unbridgeable. This polarization has been fueled by a variety of factors, including the media landscape, economic inequality, and the decline of civic institutions.

Another major challenge facing American democracy is the rise of disinformation and fake news. Social media platforms have made it easier than ever for false information to spread rapidly, often with little or no fact-checking or editorial oversight. This has contributed to a growing sense of distrust and cynicism among the American people, who are increasingly skeptical of both the media and their elected officials.

In addition to these challenges, there is also a growing threat to civil liberties in the United States. The government's surveillance programs, such as the NSA's bulk collection of phone metadata, have raised serious concerns about privacy and due process. The erosion of civil liberties is also evident in the treatment of immigrants, refugees, and other vulnerable populations, who are often subjected to discrimination and human rights abuses.

The crisis facing American democracy is urgent, and action is needed now if we are to address the root causes of the problem. One of the most important steps we can take is to promote civic engagement and a culture of democratic participation. This means not only encouraging people to vote and participate in the political process but also fostering a sense of civic duty and responsibility.

Another crucial step is to reform our political and electoral systems to make them more responsive and accountable to the needs of the American people. This includes measures such as campaign finance reform, voting rights protections, and increased transparency and accountability in government.

In addition to these specific policy proposals, there is also a need for broader cultural and social change. We need to promote media literacy and critical thinking skills so that citizens are better equipped to navigate the complex landscape of modern politics. We also need to promote a culture of empathy and compassion that recognizes the inherent dignity and worth of every human being.

The crisis facing American democracy is not a problem that can be solved by any one person or group. It requires a collective effort from all of us, as individuals and as a society. It requires us to recognize the gravity of the situation and to take action to address it. It requires us to engage in difficult conversations and to listen to those with whom we disagree. And it requires us to be willing to make the necessary sacrifices and compromises to build a stronger, more resilient democracy for the future.

The crisis facing American democracy is real, and it is urgent. We cannot afford to sit back and wait for someone else to solve the problem. We must take action now to address the root causes of the crisis and to build a stronger, more inclusive, and more resilient democracy for ourselves and future generations.

Whether through policy reforms, cultural change, or individual action, we all have a role to play in addressing this crisis and ensuring the survival of American democracy.

II. From Fracture to Unity: Bridging Political Divides

In recent years, the political divide in the United States has become deeper and more polarized than ever before. With the rise of social media and the proliferation of echo chambers, many Americans find themselves living in separate realities, with little understanding or empathy for those on the other side of the political spectrum. This division has led to a breakdown in communication and cooperation, making it difficult to solve the pressing problems facing the country.

However, there is hope for bridging this divide and bringing Americans back together. It begins with recognizing that we are all part of the same community and that we share many of the same concerns and aspirations for our country. Despite our differences, we all want to live in a safe, prosperous, and just society.

One of the key steps in bridging the political divide is to listen to one another. This means actively seeking out opposing viewpoints and engaging in respectful dialogue. We must learn to listen with an open mind, without judgment or preconceived notions. By doing so, we can begin to understand where the other side is coming from and find common ground.

Another important step is to cultivate empathy and compassion. We must recognize that those on the other side of the political divide are not our enemies but our fellow citizens, with their hopes, fears, and struggles. By putting ourselves in their shoes, we can better understand their perspective and work together to find solutions that benefit everyone.

One practical way to bridge the political divide is to focus on shared values rather than divisive issues. For example, most Americans believe in fairness, equality, and justice for all. By emphasizing these values, we can create a common framework for addressing issues such as healthcare, education, and social welfare, which are often politicized and divisive.

Another strategy is to promote collaboration and compromise. Too often, political discourse is framed as a zero-sum game, with winners and losers. However, this approach is not productive and often leads to further polarization. Instead, we must find ways to work together and seek common ground. This may mean making compromises or finding creative solutions that satisfy the needs of both sides.

In addition to these individual and collective efforts, there are also institutional and systemic changes that can help bridge the political divide. For example, we can reform the political and electoral systems to make them more representative and responsive to the needs of all Americans. This may include measures such as campaign finance reform, ranked-choice voting, and non-partisan redistricting.

We can also promote media literacy and critical thinking skills to help citizens navigate the complex landscape of modern politics. This may include promoting fact-checking and editorial standards in journalism, as well as developing programs to teach citizens how to evaluate sources and detect bias.

Bridging the political divide requires a fundamental shift in our attitudes and behaviors. We must move away from the idea that politics is a zero-sum game and embrace a more collaborative and empathetic approach. We must recognize that our differences are not insurmountable and that we share a common destiny as Americans.

Bridging the political divide is not easy, but it is essential if we are to build a stronger, more resilient democracy. By listening to one another, cultivating empathy and compassion, focusing on shared values, and promoting collaboration and compromise, we can begin to bridge the gap and work towards a brighter future for all Americans.

Whether through individual action, institutional reform, or systemic change, we all have a role to play in building a more united and inclusive country.

III. The Democratic Imperative: Restoring Trust in Institutions and Processes

In recent years, there has been a growing sense of disillusionment and distrust towards American institutions and processes. From the 2008 financial crisis to the 2020 election, many Americans have lost faith in the ability of their government and political systems to serve the needs and interests of the people.

This erosion of trust is a major threat to democracy, as it undermines the legitimacy of our political institutions and the processes that sustain them. However, there are steps we can take to restore trust and renew our commitment to democratic ideals.

One of the key ways to restore trust in democratic institutions is to ensure that they are transparent, accountable, and responsive to the needs of the people. This means promoting greater transparency in government operations and decision-making, as well as creating mechanisms for citizen participation and oversight.

Another important step is to strengthen the rule of law and the independence of the judiciary. This means ensuring that laws are applied fairly and impartially, without political interference or bias. It also means protecting the rights and freedoms of all citizens, regardless of their background or beliefs.

We must address the systemic inequalities that underlie much of the public's disillusionment with democracy. This means tackling issues such as economic inequality, racial injustice, and political polarization, which erode trust and undermine the legitimacy of our institutions.

One practical way to address these challenges is to promote greater citizen engagement and participation. This may include initiatives such as citizen assemblies, participatory budgeting, and community-led policymaking, which give citizens a greater say in the decisions that affect their lives.

Another important strategy is to promote media literacy and critical thinking skills, which can help citizens distinguish between credible and unreliable sources of information. This means teaching citizens how to evaluate evidence, recognize bias, and detect fake news and propaganda.

Restoring trust in democratic institutions requires a fundamental shift in our attitudes and values. We must move away from a culture of cynicism and apathy and embrace a more engaged, informed, and participatory approach to democracy.

This means recognizing that democracy is not a static system, but a dynamic process that requires constant attention and effort. It means committing ourselves to the ideals of transparency, accountability, and civic engagement, and working together to build a stronger, more inclusive, and more resilient democracy.

The democratic imperative to restore trust in institutions and processes is essential if we are to build a more just and equitable society. By promoting transparency, accountability, and citizen participation, as well as addressing the underlying inequalities that erode trust, we can renew our commitment to democratic ideals and build a more resilient and inclusive democracy.

Whether through individual action, institutional reform, or systemic change, we all have a role to play in ensuring the survival and vitality of our democratic institutions.

IV. Beyond the Ballot Box: The Role of Civic Engagement in a Healthy Democracy

Democracy is not just about voting. It is also about actively participating in the decisions that affect our lives, and working together to build stronger, more inclusive communities. This is where civic engagement comes in - the active involvement of citizens in the public life of their communities.

Civic engagement is a critical component of a healthy democracy, as it promotes greater accountability, transparency, and responsiveness in government, and helps to build stronger, more cohesive communities. But what exactly does civic engagement look like, and how can we encourage more of it?

At its core, civic engagement is about taking action to address the issues and challenges that matter most to us. This can take many different forms, from volunteering in our local communities to advocating for policy change at the state or national level.

One important form of civic engagement is community organizing, which involves bringing people together to address a common issue or concern. This might involve organizing a neighborhood cleanup, starting a community garden, or advocating for better public transportation in your area.

Another important form of civic engagement is advocacy, which involves speaking out on behalf of a particular cause or issue. This might involve writing letters to your elected officials, participating in public demonstrations or rallies, or engaging in social media campaigns to raise awareness and build support for your cause.

Civic engagement can also involve participating in public meetings, hearings, and other forums where citizens can express their views and concerns to government officials and other decision-makers. This can include attending city council meetings, participating in public hearings on zoning or land use issues, or testifying before a legislative committee.

The goal of civic engagement is to build stronger, more inclusive communities that are better able to address the challenges and opportunities of our times. By actively participating in the public life of our communities, we can help to shape the policies and decisions that affect our lives and build a more just, equitable, and sustainable society.

However, there are also challenges to promoting civic engagement, including issues of access, representation, and accountability. For example, certain groups - such as low-income communities, people of color, and young people - may face barriers to participating in civic life, such as lack of access to transportation, language barriers, or voter suppression.

To address these challenges, we need to promote policies and practices that promote greater access and inclusion, such as expanded voting rights, language access, and community outreach programs. We also need to ensure that our political institutions are transparent, accountable, and responsive to the needs and interests of all citizens, not just those with the most power and privilege.

Civic engagement is a vital component of a healthy democracy, as it promotes greater accountability, transparency, and responsiveness in government, and helps to build stronger, more inclusive communities. By actively participating in the public life of our communities, we can help to shape the policies and decisions that affect our lives and build a more just, equitable, and sustainable society.

However, we also need to address the challenges and barriers that prevent some groups from fully participating in civic life and work to create more accessible, inclusive, and accountable democratic institutions.

Conclusion

In conclusion, the future of American democracy presents both challenges and opportunities. The challenges include the polarization of political parties, disinformation, voter suppression, and the influence of money in politics. However, the opportunities for reform in areas such as voting rights, campaign finance, and civic engagement offer a path toward a stronger democracy.

It is crucial to learn from the past and use those lessons to guide current and future reforms. Additionally, addressing the urgent need for action is critical in restoring trust in institutions and processes. The future of American democracy depends on recognizing and addressing the challenges facing the country while also embracing the opportunities for reform.

Ultimately, a transparent, accountable, and citizen-engaged political system is necessary to ensure that the voices and needs of all Americans are represented in the political process. It is only through prioritizing these values that the future of American democracy can be strengthened and secured.